AF598645

Zoom in on Zombies

by Kari-Lynn Winters and Catherine Rondina

Fitzhenry & Whiteside

Published in Canada by Fitzhenry & Whiteside Limited,
209 Wicksteed Avenue, Unit 51, Toronto, ON M4G 0B1.
Published in the United States by Fitzhenry & Whiteside Limited,
60 Leo M Birmingham Pkwy, Ste 107, Brighton, MA 02135.

Fitzhenry & Whiteside Limited acknowledges with thanks the Canada Council for the Arts and the Ontario Arts Council for their support of our publishing program. We acknowledge the financial support of the Government of Canada through the Canada Book Fund (CBF) for our publishing activities.

Library and Archives Canada Cataloguing in Publication
Title: Zoom in on Zombies / by Kari-Lynn Winters and Catherine Rondina.
Names: Winters, Kari-Lynn, 1969- author. | Rondina, Catherine, author.
Description: Includes bibliographical references and index.
Identifiers: Canadiana 20240397401 | ISBN 9781554556083 (hardcover)
Subjects: LCSH: Animals—Miscellanea—Juvenile literature. | LCGFT: Trivia and miscellanea.
Classification: LCC QL49. .W56 2024 | DDC j591—dc23

Publisher Cataloging-in-Publication Data (U.S.)
Names: Winters, Kari-Lynn, 1969- author | Rondina, Catherine, author.
Title: Zoom in on zombies / by Kari-Lynn Winters and Catherine Rondina
Description: Toronto, Ontario : Fitzhenry & Whiteside Limited, 2024. | Summary: A look at a unique part of nature delves into the world of zombies and the many examples of natural zombies in real life, from amber snails and carpenter ants to foot fungus, wood ticks, and tardigrades" – Provided by publisher.
Identifiers: ISBN 978-1-55455-608-3 (hardcover)
Subjects: LCSH: Zombies – Juvenile literature. | Natural history – Juvenile literature. | Animals – Juvenile literature. | Insects – Juvenile literature. | BISAC: JUVENILE NONFICTION / Animals / General. | JUVENILE NONFICTION / Animals / Insects, Spiders, etc.
Classification: LCC QH48.W7878 Z87 2024 | DDC 508 – dc23

Edited by Naomi Dobler
Text and cover design by Jillian Doll
Printed in Canada by Copywell

Table of Contents

Chapter 1: Zombies Among Us 6
- Back From the Dead
- Zombie Obsessed
- Don't Freak Out
- Aaah! My Parents Are Zombies
- Stop the Zombie Tech Takeover

Chapter 2: Lame Brains and Other Zombie-Like Traits 11
- Just Your Average Zombie
- Hordes of Real-World Zombies
- A to Zombie
- How to Spot a Zombie
- Could You Be A Zombie?

Chapter 3: Feeding Frenzy 16
- What's on the Menu?
- Day of the Dead Snail
- Who's Eating Whom?
- Second Helpings

Chapter 3 continued
- Gluttonous Eaters
- Kiss of DEATH
- Exquisite Corpses
- What Devours More?

Chapter 4: Zombified 25
- Take Me to Your Larva!
- Babysitter Job Posting
- Zombie Deer Disease
- Are You Terrified by the Zombified?
- Body Snatched
- Mind Control: A Deadly Game of Mouse and Cat
- Under My Spell

Chapter 5: Dirty Rotters 33
- I'm Not Spoiled. I'm Just Rotten!
- Rotten Jokes That Really Stink
- Mmmm. The Smell of Rot!

Chapter 5 continued
- Stinkin' and Reekin'
- Rotten to the Core
- Bad to the Bone: Stages of Decay
- Rot or Not?

Chapter 6: Brain Dead 41
- Feeling Sluggish?
- A Sleep-like State
- Catching zzz's: Animal Zzz-ombies
- Dog Tired
- Dead or Asleep?
- Sleepy Treats to Die For!

Chapter 7: Zombie Moves 47
- Within 'Gaited' Communities
- Twitchy Moves
- The Zombie Shuffle Dance
- Stumbling Aimlessly
- A Mindless Wanderer
- Take Me to Your Lettuce
- Moving in Hordes and Packs

Chapter 8: Survival of the Fittest 54
- The Living Dead
- It's Alive!
- Who Will Survive?
- Mike, the Zombie-Roster Lives On!
- 10 "Never Say Die" Facts about Cockroaches
- How to Survive Natural Disasters (or a Zombie Apocalypse)

Chapter 9: Zombie Allies 61
- Maybe, Zombies Aren't So Bad?
- Munching Maggots
- Eye Spy a Zombie Plant
- Aghhhhhh. I'm Hungry
- You're a Zombie: You Haven't Aged a Bit
- Surviving Death
- You're a Zombie Survivor!

Index 67
Glossary 68
References 70
Author Bios 72

Acknowledgments

The authors would like to thank Naomi Dobler, Joyce Grant, Zabriah Dhami, Jillian Doll, Desmond Rondina Kadri, and Holly Doll "the talented zombie horde," for their undying support and brilliant BRAAAIINS!

KLW and CR

Credit

Zabriah Dhami for photo edits/illustrations.

CHAPTER 1

Zombies Among Us

BACK FROM THE DEAD

"Braaaaiins!" It's the terrifying groan of the undead (those who have died but live on). Our love of zombies is almost as odd as the creatures themselves. How did we fall prey to this genre? Simple. We like to be scared! It lets us see how other humans escape and survive.

Since the early 1900's humans have had an eerie interest in zombies as a form of entertainment. They first appeared in novels. In the 1930s zombies appeared on the big screen, for example, in Victor Halperin's *White Zombie* (1932). Additionally, movie director George A. Romero's 1968 film, *Night of the Living Dead*, is as terrifying today as it was when it first hit the movie theatres.

Later, zombies invaded the world of music, with singer Michael Jackson's 1982 famous music video, *Thriller*. Additionally, television viewers tuned in year after year, first appearing on Halloween in 2010, to learn the fate of those who fought *The Walking Dead*. And more recently, people have become entranced with zombie apocalypses in video games such as *Resident Evil* (in 1996) or *Plants Vs. Zombies* (in 2009) and in the manga series, *Highschool of the Dead* (in 2011).

Zombie fans are known as zombophiles.

ZOMBIE OBSESSED

Zombies—they seem to be everywhere! Of course, they're fictional. Originating from folklore, today you see them in TV shows, movies, video games, graphic novels, and even music videos. The writers of these media have given them zombie characteristics. Things they do and don't do. These gross looking beings shuffle around aimlessly, always in search of human brains, which is apparently their favourite meal. They also moan and twitch, while pieces of their bodies rot off. They are the "living dead" and they need to feed off others to survive. Killing them is hard to do, because blows to the limbs, guts, or heart don't work. Even drowning won't slay them. The only way to kill a zombie is through decapitation (removing its head) or permanently damaging the infected brain.

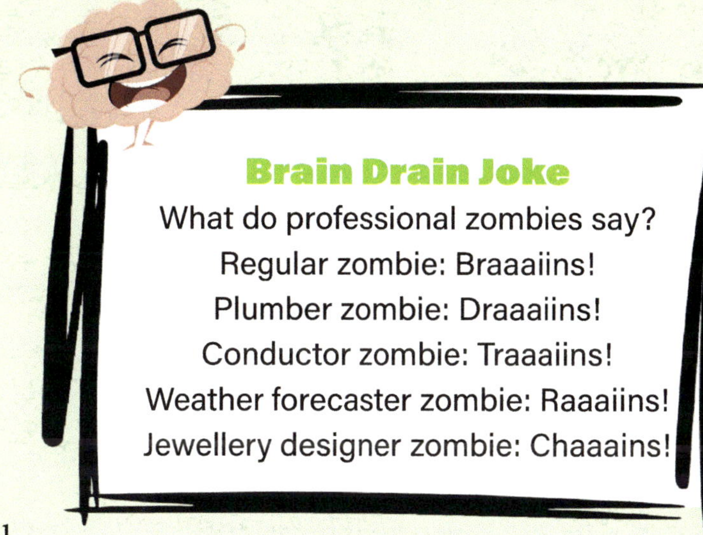

And, beware, these undead corpses have insatiable appetites for flesh, and especially brains! If you become their victim, you will become **zombified**—turned into a zombie! When this happens, we know that one of two things must have occurred. Either you have been bitten directly by a zombie or a zombie's blood touched your skin. We don't actually know what it is that makes these undead capable of spreading their condition to humans. It could be an infection. Or possibly a virus. Whatever the cause, once you've been infected, one thing is for sure—you'll be bodysnatched and under their control. Now you're one of them!

October 8th is World Zombie Day–Get your FREAK on!

DON'T FREAK OUT

So, everything you've read and heard about zombies seems unlikely, right? Yeah, scientists have made it clear that these living-dead characters aren't real. Phew—that's a relief!

But before you pack away your zombie survival kit, check this out. In March 2021, people surfing the internet were shocked to discover a blog post from the Centers for Disease Control and Prevention (CDC) in Atlanta, Georgia. The article, called, "Preparedness 101: Zombie **Apocalypse**," was found on the CDC's Public Health Matters blog, where it was originally posted way back in 2011.

No biggie right? Wrong! The CDC is an official government agency in the United States. Its main purpose is to watch over the health, safety and potential security threats of its U.S. citizens. People around the world use this very important information provided by the CDC to make serious decisions when it comes to matters that could affect us all, such as natural disasters and pandemics. So imagine when the warning to prepare yourself for a possible zombie apocalypse was posted—a lot of people started freaking out!

Luckily for us the blog post turned out to be just a prank the CDC set up to grab people's attention and make them more aware of the importance of planning ahead for any emergency that could develop. Not funny, CDC!

AAAH! MY PARENTS ARE ZOMBIES!

Though the CDC blog post was meant to be funny, there appears to be real-life zombies in your own home. It's true! Keep an eye on your parents. You'll spot them shuffling around in a trance-like state or wandering aimlessly bent over a smartphone or tablet. Easily distracted, they bump into other family members, unaware of those around them. Sound familiar?

Sure does. It's the takeover of handheld electronic devices, and it's already got your parents zombified! It tells them when to wake up, where to go, how to get to where they are going, what they will see along the way, and even when they have arrived. It helps them monitor your house, make online banking transactions, and find their favourite meals! Could the zombie takeover have already begun?

Yes! Every year, more and more people become slaves to their phones. Recently, scientists studying the attention spans of electronic device users discovered that Canadians are losing their ability to focus! Their findings demonstrated a steady decline in the number of seconds it takes for the average human to become distracted. In 2000, the average Canadian could only concentrate their attention for 12 seconds. By 2013, these tech-zombies had slipped even further into a mind fog, only being able to focus for eight seconds. Pretty scary when you realize that a goldfish is thought to have a nine second attention span! Wonder what the year 2030 has in store for us?

STOP THE ZOMBIE TECH TAKEOVER

Could your parents be zombified?
It's not too late to save them!

3:10 PM

TRY THIS

The Dead Zone –Stare at your parents until they notice. When they see you, pretend to play dead. When they ask what you are doing, say, "For the next 30 minutes, we are in the dead zone and NO computers, phones, or tablets are allowed."

Body Snatch – Tell your parents that their minds are now under your control. Suggest a family walk to get an ice cream treat. Remind them that while under your command—handheld devices stay out of sight.

Dawn of the Silence – Zombies are attracted to sound. So when your parent's phone rings or one of them starts talking or texting, give them the zombie stare and shamble towards them.

CHAPTER 2

Lame Brains and Other Zombie-Like Traits

JUST YOUR AVERAGE ZOMBIE

Zombies are a hardy lot, with distinct characteristics; these lame brains are dazed, confused, and often speechless. Hungry for flesh, they are rotten to the core and persistent survivors.

Zombies have other identifiable traits, too. To be bitten by a zombie would result in **stupefaction**—a state of being unable to think! Though they appear sleep deprived or brain dead, they rarely tire. Even when they're missing body parts, they twitch, jerk, or stumble forward, usually without any emotion. Indeed, their mindless, hobbling movements indicate that they are driven by thoughtless urges. But this couldn't happen in real life… could it?

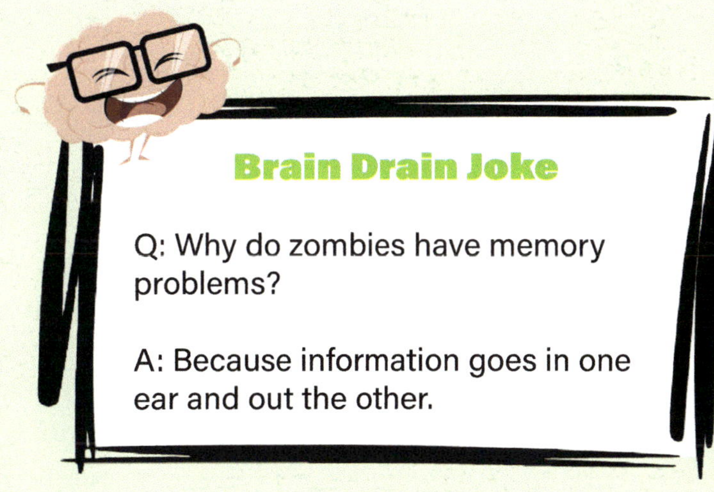

HORDES OF REAL-WORLD ZOMBIES

Hordes of actual zombies are among us, but not the TV kind. Real-life creatures with zombie qualities exist on every continent on Earth, even Antarctica.

Some, like Komodo dragons, are persistent and seemingly mindless predators. These massive lizards have been known to stalk their prey for days before devouring every bit of it, including its organs, hide, hooves, and bones.

Others, like Guinea worms and Hairworms, compel the people, animals, or insects they live in–their hosts–to hurl themselves into bodies of water.

Still others, like the Sacculina carcini (an ocean **barnacle** found on crabs) or the Parasitoid wasp, body-snatch their victims to either steal their energy, prevent them from having their own babies, or worse… to eat them alive.

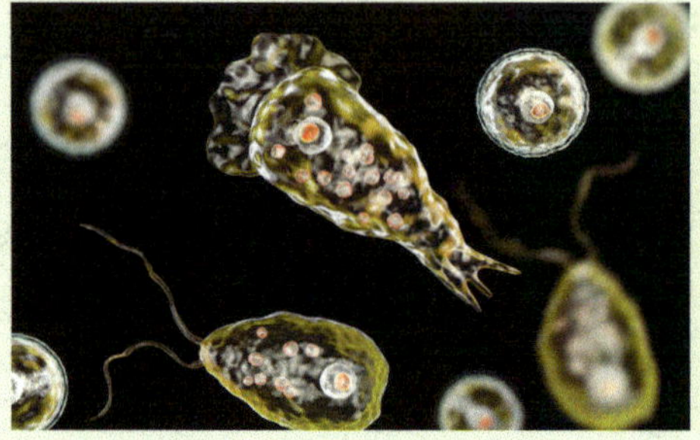

And some, like the Naegleria fowleri (a single-celled organism) and the Liver fluke (a small worm), which are both parasitic, meddle with their host's brain and alter their behaviour. Lurking in forests, jungles, meadows, and murky bodies of water, the creepers, fliers, and swimmers in this book are rotten to the core.

Natural zombies are everywhere.

Here is a list of real-world zombies. Stay tuned as we unearth more facts about these creatures in the following chapters that will make you squirm.

A TO ZOMBIE

Check out this A-Z list of nature's smelly, slow-moving, parasitic, or carnivorous real-world beings that come with zombie-like traits.

Amber snails (when zombified, they twitch their eye stalks)
Baker's yeast (returns to life 100+ years after dormancy)
Carpenter ants (wander aimlessly when bodysnatched)
Deadly nightshade (turns a human into a slurring lamebrain)
E coli (feasts on human or animal guts)
Foot **fungus** (feeds on rotting flesh)
Guinea worms (compel humans to plunge into water)
Horsehair worms (brainwash **hosts** to drown themselves)
Inland taipan snakes (deliver a deadly bite)
Jewel wasps (stupify and control their prey)
Komodo dragons (stalk their prey for days)
Liver **flukes** (enter human bile ducts, causing energy loss)
Maggots (gnaw on living tissue)
Naegleria fowleri (eat human brains)
Ophiocordyceps **fungi** (body snatch their victims)
Parasitoid wasps (convert victims into cocoon defenders)
Q fever **bacteria** (make their livestock hosts sleepy)
Rabies Virus (makes victims twitch and wander aimlessly)
Sacculina carcini (body snatch crabs and steal their energy)
Tardigrades (die of dehydration and then revive themselves)
Unau sloths (are slow-moving and oblivious to temperature)
Venus flytraps (devour their prey live)
Wood ticks (detect hosts by their odour and movement)
Xoplasma Gondii (drives rodents to run towards cats)
Yucca Moths (survive the harshest environments)
Zorillas (smell worse than rotting flesh)

Amber Snail

Parasitoid Wasp

Look for these natural zombies throughout the book!

Tardigrade

Venus Flytraps

HOW TO SPOT A ZOMBIE

Match up the labelled illustrations of real-world zombies with their zombie-like traits.

1. Zombies smell terrible–worse than rotting flesh. This African weasel is one of the worst-smelling creatures on Earth.

2. Zombies flail and twitch. If you see this animal acting strangely—standing on its back legs, foaming at the mouth and shuffling forward—it might have a viral disease called rabies.

3. Zombies have insatiable appetites. This aquatic creature eats over 40 million krill and crustaceans a day.

4. Zombies deliver a painful bite. When this viper attacks it releases a venom that can dissolve flesh.

5. Zombies devour brains. This reptile hunts down its prey and swallows it whole (including the prey's brains, hide, bones, and guts). Its forked tongue can detect an injured victim up to 8 km (five miles) away.

6. Zombies are called the living dead. Some say the disease caused by this blood-feeding insect can live for more than 20 years in a human body, possibly leading to that person's death.

Answer Key:
Raccoon=2; Blue Whale=3; Zorilla=1; Komodo Dragon=5; Kissing Bug=6; Bushmaster Snake=4

COULD YOU BE A ZOMBIE?

Answer the following questions – if you dare!

1. Have you ever been "dead tired" on a Monday morning?
2. Is your morning breath so rotten your dog hides under the covers?
3. Do you drag yourself out of bed at the start of the day?
4. Is it an effort to shuffle to the bathroom and get yourself ready for school?
5. Does your mouth gape open when you devour your breakfast?
6. Do you find yourself moaning and groaning when your teacher hands out homework?
7. Have you ever aimlessly followed people on social media?
8. Do you greedily feast on your favourite meal, gobbling up more than one helping?
9. Have you ever let a stinky one rip, and then blamed your best friend?
10. Do you find yourself gaming into the wee hours of the night (the graveyard shift) on the weekends?

What was your score?
YIKES!

Chapter 3

Feeding Frenzy

WHAT'S ON THE MENU?

One thing we've learned from the invasion of zombies on television, in movies, and in video games, is they like to eat. But who doesn't? Did you know that every real-life living creature on the planet needs to eat? Even plants, bacteria, viruses, and **parasites**!

Living things need **nutrients**–substances such as vitamins and minerals–to survive. It's nature's way. From the majestic maple trees to the tiniest woodland wildflowers. From squirrels, rabbits, and foxes to snakes, turtles, and lizards. From turkey vultures, fish, and beetles to tapeworms, mushrooms, and even bacteria like E-coli. All these living things rely on other living things for nourishment, making them all part of something called an **ecosystem**.

Each living thing offers nutrients and energy to another hungry creature in that ecosystem. For instance, imagine a rabbit munching on the forest floor, eating grasses. This rabbit might become a hawk's next meal. When this hawk dies, fungi and bacteria will decompose (break down) the hawk's corpse.

These helpful **microorganisms** release a chemical called Nitrogen, which the soil may be lacking. This chemical helps the grasses (that the rabbits and other herbivores munched on) become thicker and healthier. And so the energy cycle continues. Some people call this energy cycle a "food chain".

A food chain is continuous. For example, a food chain may look like this:

or like this…

But a food chain can also weave with another food chain.

Zombie Bites

Owls, like komodo dragons, regurgitate gastric pellets of indigestible materials after consuming prey whole, including feathers, bones, and fur.

DAY OF THE DEAD SNAIL

When Mother Nature asked an amber snail (*Succineidae*) to dance, it should have replied, "*No thanks, I'll sit this one out.*" Little did the snail know that it would wind up getting bodysnatched by little flatworms and made to perform zombie-like moves that would lead to its demise. Talk about killin' it on the dance floor!

So how do these worm-like parasites transform that snail into a dancing zombie? Well, this strange encounter begins when an amber snail eats bird poop, containing the microscopic eggs of a type of tiny flatworm known as *Leucochloridium paradoxum*. Once inside the snail's stomach, these eggs hatch. The hatched **larvae** eventually find their way to the **eyestalks** (the protruding body parts that look like antennae) on the top of the amber snail's head.

The tiny worm-like larvae move about, causing the snail's eyestalks to bulge and throb. The flatworms now have the snail under their control! In this zombified state the snail goes out into the daylight (something it would almost never do, normally). The dancing zombie is now an easy target for hungry birds looking for a meal.

Unfortunately, that's not the end of this gruesome tale. Any unlucky bird who eats the snail's eyestalks, now has worms in its guts. Before long, the bird poops out the parasite eggs and larvae, to be eaten by other amber snails. And the whole process–including the zombie dance–begins again!

Bird poop containing Leucochloridium paradoxum

Amber Snail

Bird eating an infected amber snail

WHO'S EATING WHOM?

Imagine yourself sitting on a riverbank, fishing with your best friend. It's a perfect afternoon and you patiently wait for your first nibble. Your stomach rumbles. Mmm, fried fish is your favourite!

Suddenly, your line starts to pull—you've got something! "Reel it in!" your buddy yells, as he grabs the net to haul in your catch. Just as you see that shimmering beauty break the surface, a huge bird swoops from the sky and grabs your fish in mid-air. And the food chain continues.

From the list below, determine five living things that are not a part of a freshwater **food web**.

Herons
Bacteria
Alligators
Whales
Water striders
Tuna
Crayfish

Frogs
Sea Turtles
Algae
Urchins
Carp
Dragonflies
Mosquitos

Coral
Leeches
Earthworms
Goldfish
Salamanders
Catfish
Water snakes

Answer Key:
Coral, Sea Turtles, Tuna, Urchins, Whales

SECOND HELPINGS

Zombies are all about feeding their never-ending appetites. But what drives them to devour? You might be surprised to learn that it's likely the same thing that has you going back to the all-you-can-eat buffet at your favourite restaurant. That's right—it has everything to do with your brain!

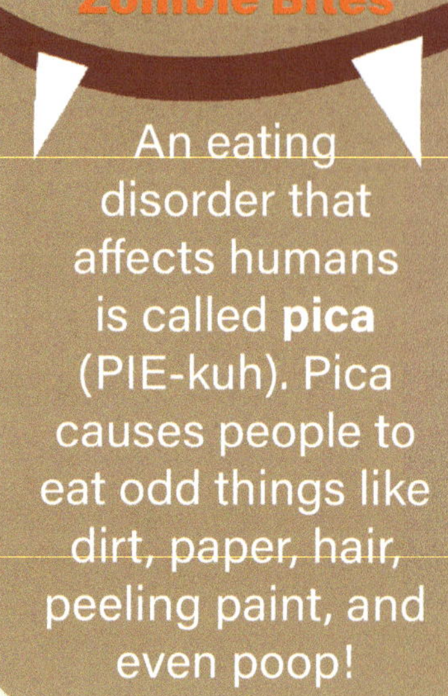

Zombie Bites

An eating disorder that affects humans is called **pica** (PIE-kuh). Pica causes people to eat odd things like dirt, paper, hair, peeling paint, and even poop!

Not brains to eat. What are you—a zombie? But the brain that controls everything you do. The feeling of hunger comes from a gland within your brain, called the hypothalamus. This gland initiates two functions.

1. It makes you feel full.
2. It makes you feel hungry.

The fictional world of zombies suggests that these walking corpses must have active hypothalamus glands, because they are always hungry!

GLUTTONOUS EATERS

Hippos – Can eat up to 40 kg (88 lbs) of grasses, leaves, fruits, and aquatic plants each night. Talk about late night snackers.

Grizzly bears – May devour 40-50 kg (80-90 lbs) of their favourite foods, like roots, grasses, insects, fish and even human garbage daily!

Giraffes – Consume almost 34 kg (74 lbs) of their preferred meal–leaves, each day! Their diet may also include grasses, fruits and vegetables.

Buffalos – Gobble down 10 kg (24 lbs) of grass, weeds, and woody plants, per day!

Rhinos – Known to eat up to 32 different species of plants daily, these large mammals ingest 68 kg (150 lbs) of grass, shrubs, trees and roots to satisfy their appetite.

Ladybugs have an insatiable appetite for aphids—small green insects that feed on plants. Adult ladybugs eat all day long, and probably eat close to 50 aphids daily.

Female wood ticks—also known as American dog ticks—drink a lot of blood and get huge—100 times their original weight. That would be like a human ballooning to the size of an elephant!

KISS OF DEATH

It's called the "praying mantis" because of the way its legs fold up to its face. It looks like it's praying. Maybe what it's praying for is ... living things to eat! Just like a zombie that feeds on living beings, a praying mantis' favourite food is alive. It will eat dead insects, but that's definitely a distant second. Even though praying mantises mostly prey on creeping spiders and crawling insects, they won't turn down frogs, and will even eat birds!

It's their sneaky style that makes them sly predators. Their green or brown colouring allows them to hide in grassy and leafy surroundings. Praying mantises are **diurnal**, meaning they only hunt in the daytime and can keep perfectly still for hours, waiting for their next victim to come along. But, once they're ready to attack, they can react in less than a tenth of a second!

But wait... there's something even more fascinating—and gross—about the praying mantis.

It eats its partner's brain (or in zombie terms—its **braaaain**!)

The male praying mantis often approaches the female, climbing up on her back. It's during this act of reproduction that the female decides it's snack time! She will turn her head and start chomping away on her partner's brain—while he is still alive. Scientists have discovered that female praying mantises who eat these brains, immediately after the mating process is done, tend to produce more eggs.

Aw, how nice! What a good mother. She does it all for the children.

EXQUISITE CORPSES: DRAWING EXERCISE

Try drawing a new breed of zombie from some of nature's feasting creatures. Using the examples below, invent your own all-consuming ghoul.

- California condor vulture—who eats dead and rotting meat, and whose wings extend to 3 metres (that's almost 10 feet!).
- Saki monkey—whose canine teeth are pointy and sharp, able to break through nut shells and fruit rinds.
- Pipevine swallowtail caterpillar—once fully mature, can tip the scales at 2,700 times their hatched weight!
- Argentine Horned Frog—whose large mouths make up 50% of their body size! Better to eat you with, my dear.
- Burmese Python—is one of the largest snakes on earth! Weighing in at 90 kg (200 lbs) it likes to chow down on pigs, goats and even alligators! A fully grown adult can reach up to 7 metres (23 feet).

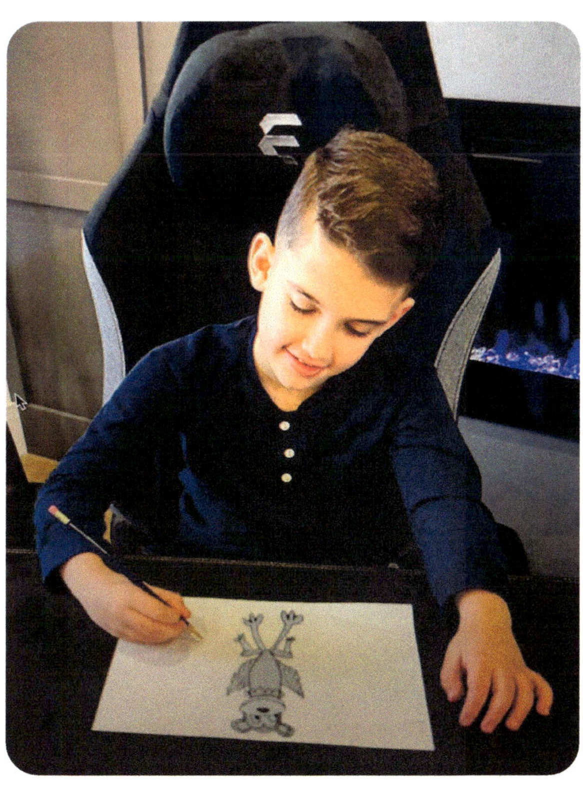

WHAT DEVOURS MORE?: MATCH-UP QUIZ

1. Fastest eater, ploughing through dirt for earthworms and leeches at breakneck speed!

2. Spending most of their time wandering around looking for food, these adult animals consume nearly 136 kg (300 pounds) of grasses and leaves a day!

3. Eating three times its body weight per day, this rodent can only live without food for two hours.

4. This underwater nightmare can grow just over 5 metres (18 feet) in length and never says no to a meal!

5. These tiny night-raiders consume one-third of their body weight on an average evening out. That's almost 3000 insects a night!

6. Weighing between 2–20 grams (0.08-0.8 ounces), these speedy birds eat almost three times their weight every day!

7. This river dweller prefers to eat plants, but even eating mostly greens doesn't keep its weight down!

8. This picky eater is the largest animal on earth.

Star-Nosed Mole 2. African Elephant 3. Pygmy
rew 4. Tiger Shark 5. Little Brown Bat
Hummingbird 7. Hippopotamus 8. Blue Whale

Chapter 4

Zombified

TAKE ME TO YOUR LARVA!

Would you leave your children in the care of a zombie babysitter?
No?

Well, that's exactly what a parasitic wasp (*Dinocampus Coccinellae*), does when it takes control of a ladybug. In fact, it turns the ladybug into a brainwashed caregiver for its eggs. In this way, the green-eyed wasp is wicked and clever. She uses her stinger to inject a single wasp egg, along with a virus, into the underbelly of the ladybug. As the wasp egg grows, so does the virus, living in the tissues that surround the egg.

The ladybug unknowingly carries this horrible hitchhiker (and virus) for nearly three weeks in its tummy. Eventually, the egg ruptures and a wasp larva appears. Hungry, the wriggly worm-like larva feasts on the ladybug's guts and eventually eats its way out through the ladybug's exoskeleton—its hard, outer shell. This feasting doesn't kill the ladybug, but the virus starts to take over the bug's brain.

The ladybug tries to fight off the virus on its own, but is usually unsuccessful. The ladybug often ends up temporarily paralyzed. Then, the wasp larva spins a cocoon between the ladybug's legs, entrapping it even further. The imprisoned and zombified ladybug is forced to stay put. Confused, this ladybug fights any predator (e.g., spiders, beetles) that comes near the larva, making the ladybug an ideal caregiver and bodyguard for the wasp.

Brain Drain Joke

Why won't that ladybug stand up for herself?

Answer: She doesn't have the guts.

Babysitter Job Posting (A Brain Drain Classified Ad)

WANTED

I am *Dinocampus Coccinellae* (aka: wasp). I am looking for a babysitter to watch over my precious larva for three weeks this spring.
Must haves:

- Only lady(bugs) need to apply.
- Be able to stay calm even when your gut feeling is eating at you.
- Must be selfless and open to sharing your inner being.

Though you may have had previous babysitting duties with parasitic wasps, no experience is necessary.

Your duties will include:

- Opening yourself to new experiences.
- Hosting family gatherings.
- Providing meals for my young one.
- Ensuring my baby's safety from predators.

If you feel you are the right fit,
email me at
zombiewasp@hotmeal.com

REPLY:

Dear Ms. D. Coccinellae (may I call you wasp?),

I am Coccinellidae Septempunctata (aka: Ladybug). I am applying for the nanny position you advertised in the Arthropod Daily Times.

You can trust me to be an excellent babysitter for your precious little one.

I am a protective, homebody, who will guard your home (cocoon) and never fly away.

As a mother of hundreds of larvae myself, I am an experienced caregiver and a generous host, especially for family gatherings—I love little squirmers! Your offspring will never go hungry when I am around. I will provide nourishing meals and will ensure it eats well for all three weeks. In closing, I am open to new experiences and I look forward to accommodating all of your family's needs.

With all my heart,
Ms. Coccinellidae Septempunctata

Zombie Bites

The phobia of being zombified is called kinemortophobia (kin-uh-mawr-tuh-foh-bee-uh).

ZOMBIE DEER DISEASE

For more than 50 years, a brain disease has been turning forests in North America into a type of Zombieland. Deer, elk, reindeer and moose have been roaming the woodlands, infected with Zombie Deer Disease. Also known as Chronic Wasting Disease (CWD), this brain-eating infection slowly turns strong, healthy animals (especially those from the deer family) into zombies. The transformation can take time to get its grasp on a creature. It can take more than a year or two before the horrific symptoms of the disease begin to show!

The first sign of the illness is dramatic weight-loss in the animal. The deer, elk, reindeer, or moose may also shake uncontrollably, appear to have a glazed look in its eyes, wander without knowing where it is, and lack any fear of humans. It becomes the walking dead—awaiting its inevitable death.

But how do these animals contract this deadly disease? When eating grass, the animals sometimes ingest infected soil that contains microscopic germs (or **pathogens**) that invade the animals' bodies and make them sick. These can be bacteria, viruses, *parasites* or fungi and they determine the type of sickness. For Zombie Deer Disease (CWD), scientists debate the exact *pathogen* that causes the deterioration of the animals. What is known is that these microorganisms cannot be destroyed! They take over, explode, and create microscopic holes in the brain. Once this infection occurs, the deer's brain now appears to resemble a sponge, rather than a living organ.

Sadly, there are no vaccines, or any form of treatment to stop or control Zombie Deer Disease—it is always deadly. While the disease has never been found in humans, experts caution that it could soon become a health issue for people, too.

ARE YOU TERRIFIED BY THE ZOMBIFIED?

Real world zombie dominators come in many shapes and sizes, some with the intention to brainwash their victims. Using a scale of 1-5–with 1 being the least scary and 5 being the most terrifying—rate the experiences of the zombified creatures below.

________ Experiencing blistering heat inside your leg. Guinea worms infect drinking water. Once a human drinks this contaminated water, the Guinea worms mate in the host's stomach. Though the male worms die soon after mating, the female worms live and grow to become nearly one metre (three feet) long. The pregnant Guinea worm, needing water to release her eggs, travels down the human leg and releases blazing hot chemicals. This burning feeling compels the human to race into a nearby lake or stream.

________ Drowning yourself. Crickets, if they eat an infected insect, can become the victim of a Horsehair worm. These long, thin worms, that grow up to one metre (three feet) in length, chomp on their hosts' brain, in hopes of hitching a ride to a lake or stream. Once there, the cricket becomes a brainwashed, suicidal lunatic! Though the cricket can't swim, it hurls itself into its watery grave.

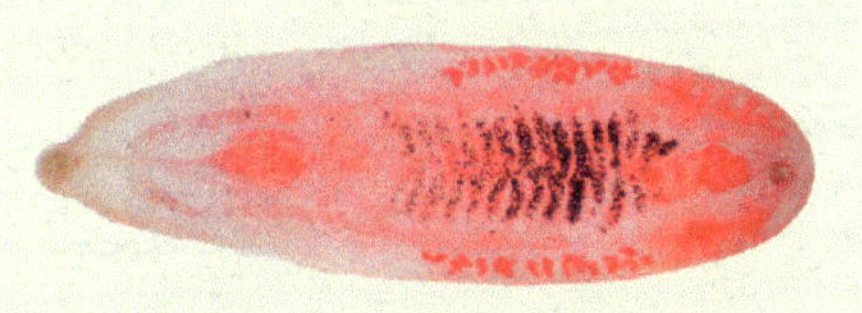

________ Being eaten alive. Flukes manipulate Killifish behaviour. These flatworms, after entering the gills of fish, force their victims to swim on their side and flash their silver underbelly. Birds can now spot these fish, scoop them out of the water, and eat them alive.

________ Allowing a worm-like larva to squirm beneath your skin. Botflies attach themselves to mosquitos and lay their eggs. When the mosquito lands on a person, these Botfly eggs fall off and hatch into larvae. Next, these newly hatched insects burrow deep into the human's body, wriggle around, and feed on human flesh for five to ten weeks.

BODY SNATCHED

After paralyzing a cockroach with her powerful sting, the female Jewel Wasp then zombifies it with her state-of-the-art surgical skills. Specifically, her stinger has miniature receptors that sense tension and pressure. Thus, with great precision she is able to insert her stinger and then inject venom in exactly the right spot in the cockroach's brain—making her prisoner completely cooperative. The cockroach is so zombified at this point that the Jewel Wasp will eat the cockroach's antennae, drag it around (by its newly broken antennae stubs), and feed her young wasp larvae without any fight from her victim.

Zombie Bites

The jewel wasp isn't the only insect that can turn others into zombies. The Zatypota Wasp can make a mean spider turn into a servant-zombie with just one sting.

MIND CONTROL: A DEADLY GAME OF MOUSE AND CAT

It's classic cartoon action - cat chases mouse, mouse outsmarts cat, and mouse escapes unharmed. Sounds like a typical Saturday morning adventure, right? Not always. In the real-life zombified world of cat and mouse, the mouse's tale may not end so happily ever after.

So you might ask, "What would make a mouse befriend a cat?" A mouse, when eating plants, may accidentally consume contaminated soil containing a parasite. This parasite called Toxoplasma Gondii (Tok-so-plaz-ma Gôn-dee) turns mice into zombies. Specifically, once inside a mouse, the parasite causes **cysts** (balls of fluid or pus) to form, which press against this rodent's brain and cause it to act strangely. As this happens, the infected mouse loses its instinctive fear of cats (and other predators)! The mouse no longer runs away from the cat; instead it is now attracted to the cat, and especially the scent of the cat's urine.

If the cat eats that zombie mouse, it, too, will be infected, but will show no signs of the disease. The parasite will, however, breed inside the kitty's intestines and will be pooped out. This further spreads the disease.

Mice and cats aren't the only warm-blooded animals that can be hosts for the Toxoplasma gondii parasite—humans can too!

It is estimated that one-third of us two-legged beings test positive for the infection. The disease is commonly contracted by touching kitty litter, (cat poop), eating meat that has not been thoroughly cooked, or drinking contaminated water.

While this parasite normally causes mild infections in people, who experience flu-like symptoms, it can become very serious in some cases. For example, studies have linked the parasite infection to mental illnesses like Schizophrenia. Moreover, compelling evidence from Johns Hopkins University shows that people with Schizophrenia are two to three times more likely to have parasite antibodies (meaning their bodies tried to fight out a parasitic infection at some point in their lives).

Historically studies show this disease has been traced in humans all the way back to ancient Egyptian times (nearly 30 centuries ago). So unless this pathogen gets destroyed, it seems that this game of mouse and cat may continue for decades to come.

UNDER MY SPELL

In this chapter we've begun exploring how different living creatures can become zombified, having their bodies or their minds taken over. While the idea might seem unlikely in real-life, especially for humans, don't shut your brain off just yet.

Mind control, or brainwashing, is a very real occurrence and you've probably had your brain manipulated a few times! If you've ever watched a TV commercial and thought—I want that, I'd eat that, or I have to have that, then you've been brainwashed! Truthfully, we all have. This form of brainwashing is found in advertising all the time. In fact, companies design psychological tricks to make us want to buy their products or services.

Consumers have become so familiar with the product's name and logo that they purchase these snacks without even needing to be told what's inside. That's mind control!

For example, a well-known corn chip brand doesn't even have to put their name or their logo on their bags anymore - just a simple triangle is all they use to get you craving those tasty Doritos™.

Think you can develop a mind controlling product that will have zombified buyers eating out of your hands? Try the activity below.

Create your own brand of potato chips.
Here are some tips to help you zombify your customers.

- Think of a clever product name to attract buyers.
- Design a brilliant logo—what will your colours be?
- Draw a visual representation of your product (be sure to include your logo).
- Develop a catchy phrase or tagline for your brand.
- Generate a marketing plan that will have customers mindlessly devouring your product.

Chapter 5

Dirty Rotters

I'M NOT SPOILED. I'M JUST ROTTEN!

Ew, what stinks? A rotting zombie? The walking dead? No, it's a living animal! Some of the smelliest real-life creatures on the planet are skunks, polecats, stink bugs, musk oxen, stinkbirds, and opossums. Why do these stinkers smell so foul? There are reasons for the different stenches.

For skunks, polecats, and stink bugs, their foul smells are their secret defence weapons. For example, skunks have scent glands under their tails that produce a yellow oil called thiol. This oily compound is not pee, nor is it a fart. Thiol smells awful. That's because it contains a stinky substance called sulfur. Skunks, polecats, and stink bugs are only some of nature's creatures that spray putrid-smelling liquids to keep their enemies away.

On the other hand, male musk oxen mark their territory by peeing on patches of grass. At first their urine smells sweet. However, over time, and as it gets trapped in their long underbelly fur, it turns foul-smelling—at least to the human nose. Believe it or not, female musk oxen like the smell of the male's urine. In fact, the females often find their mates by their scent!

Stinkbirds reek like manure. That's because of their unusual diet (swampy plant matter—leaves, fruits and flowers) and because of the slow speed in which their food breaks down in their gut (up to 45 hours per meal). By the time the food has been digested, it has fermented or soured.
Yum! Imagine how delightful this smell would be: like the tangy, earthy scent of rancid, souring, decaying leaves!

Opossums smell like decaying corpses! First, like true zombies, these critters will eat just about anything—ticks, dead birds, and even the bones of snakes. So their breath smells disgusting! Pee-ew! And if their bad breath isn't smelly enough to ward off enemies (e.g., a coyote or fox), when opossums sense danger they play dead, lying down and staying very still. Then, they secrete a putrid odour from their bum. The awful smell makes the fox or coyote think that the opossum is already dead. Not wanting to eat an already dead animal, the predator moves on.

So what is the stinkiest living critter on earth? No one knows. Even scientists cannot agree. I guess it depends on whose nose is doing the smelling.

Brain Drain Jokes

How do you keep a possum from smelling?

Hold its nose.

What are the favourite vegetables of the walking dead?

Zombeets

Kari: Hey Cathy, if a musk oxen smells musky and a stink bug smells stinky, how does a polecat smell?

Cathy: With its nose, of course!

MMMM. THE SMELL OF ROT!

Komodo dragons are on the hunt for flesh—dead or alive! These giant lizards don't use their noses to smell. They use their sensitive tongues! Their long, forked tongues can smell a dying animal (e.g., water buffalo) from four kilometres (2.5 miles) away, and they will instinctively follow it for up to four days.

Since 1969, thanks to the research of an American biologist (Walter Auffenberg), people believed that the komodo dragon had rot-inducing bacteria in its saliva—bacteria that was so deadly, it could debilitate and kill a water buffalo.

More recently, however, this myth has been debunked. Dr. Brian Fry, a researcher from the University of Queensland, discovered in 2009 that though komodo dragons do have venom glands that produce a deadly venom, their saliva is surprisingly ordinary. In fact, Dr. Fry explains that a komodo dragon's drool is similar to most other predators' saliva. In fact, it is the water buffalo's habits that actually aid in their own rotting demise. When wounded, water buffalo will seek warm water to soothe their wounds. However, the water they seek to stand in is often stagnant and brimming with harmful bacteria. These rank water holes make the water buffalo sicker, eventually bringing them down and causing death.

STINKIN' AND REEKIN'

Play this game with your friends. Start by determining the boundaries of your playing area. In the centre of the room place a chair. Make the outside boundary the "least stinkin'" zone and make the chair the "most reekin'" zone. Have a leader call out rotten-smelling things like wet dog or sweaty hockey gear. Players listen to the leader's calls then move their bodies closer to or further from the chair—depending on how stinkin' and reekin' they judge the foul thing to be. Here are some rank examples to get you started.

- Cow farts
- Gasoline
- Rotting fish
- Garlic
- Skunk spray
- Musk oxen pee
- Spoiled meat
- A friend's socks after a hockey game
- Decaying zombie flesh
- Rotten eggs
- Permanent markers

Zombie Bites

Leave the pit in your guacamole—it keeps the avocado from turning brown and it looks better to eat!

Zombie Bites

Bananas and berries are the fruits that rot the fastest, due to their high sugar content.

Zombie Bites

The stinking corpse lily is considered by some to be the world's smelliest plant, emitting odours of decaying corpses mixed with smelly socks and rotten fish.

ROTTEN TO THE CORE

It's the last day of school and Brendan is excited, but also hungry. On the bus ride home, he takes a big bite of his fresh, green apple. Afraid to get caught eating on the bus, he tosses that half-eaten apple into his backpack. At home, forgetting about the apple, Brendan throws his backpack under his bed and says hello to summer.

Within hours, the bitten part of Brendan's apple starts turning brown. That's because it is rotting (**oxidizing**). There are three things that are needed to make apples rot . The first is an enzyme (made from **proteins**) called phenolase. These proteins are also found in other fruits and vegetables, including peaches, pears, apricots, bananas, mushrooms, avocados, and lettuce. Second, you need a **catalyst** (a chemical substance) that causes a reaction. This substance remains unchanged after the reaction. For apples, their catalysts are tiny molecules called phenols. All apple cells contain phenolase (the **enzymes** that are made from proteins) and phenols (the catalysts). Third, you need oxygen.

As the half-eaten apple gets exposed to air (oxygen), it begins to break down. The more the phenolase, phenols, and oxygen come in contact with each other, the faster the flesh of the fruit begins to rot.

By early July, that apple's firm and shiny skin starts to wrinkle and shrivel. And all the while, the brown rot spreads throughout the apple's insides. When phenolase, phenols, and oxygen interact, a chemical called Melanin, a brown protein, is newly produced.

The rot will continue to take over what remains of the apple until it no longer has access to phenols or oxygen. In September when Brendan prepares to start school again, all he will find is a fuzzy, shrivelled, revolting pile of ick.

BAD TO THE BONE: STAGES OF DECAY

After a person dies, their body goes through four stages of decomposition (breaking down).

Stage 1: Fresh
(zero to 72 hours after death)

Immediately after death, excess Carbon Dioxide (the gas that people breathe out) in the cells causes cell membranes to burst open and set free enzymes, which destroy the body.

Stage 2: Bloat
(Two to five days after death)

The enzymes also produce gases, causing the body to discolour and swell to twice its normal size. This stage of the decay process is very stinky.

Stage 3: Active Decay
(Five-30 days after death)

Fluids are released from the organs, skin, and muscles through bodily orifices (e.g., nostrils or mouth). The body loses a lot of mass during this stage. Insect activity begins to happen as maggots and beetles feed on the dead body.

Stage 4: Skeletonization
(one month to several years, depending on the corpse's environment)

Since the body now has less mass, the decay process slows down. Still, it continues to decompose until only the bones and teeth remain.

Zombie Bites

Nutrient-rich soil can turn a skeleton into dust and dirt in about 20 years. However, in neutral soil, like sand, bones can stay intact for hundreds of years.

ROT OR NOT?

Try this deterioration experiment.
Have you heard that Twinkies™ never rot?
Perhaps because they are made with **preservatives** (chemicals used to keep food fresh). Some people wonder if these cake-like treats can survive a nuclear war or a zombie apocalypse. What do you think?
Try this six-step science experiment and find out for yourself.

Step 1: Ask a Question
Here are examples of questions you might ask, "Do Twinkies™ rot?" or "Will Twinkies™ rot in different environments?"

Step 2: Do Some Background Research
Take a closer look at the ingredients of Twinkies™.
https://www.hostesscakes.com/
Do these ingredients appear natural to you? Do all natural ingredients rot?

Step 3: Make a Guess
Given the information that you have researched, answer your initial question.
For example, "I think the Twinkies™ will rot".

Step 4: Let's Try it!

You Will Need:

- Twinkies™ (at least 4)
- 2 glass jars with lids
- 2 plates
- Water
- Aluminum foil (enough to wrap one Twinkie™)

What to do:

1. Place one Twinkie™ on a plate.
2. Wrap another Twinkie™ in aluminum foil. Place it on a plate.
3. Put a third Twinkie™ in a jar. Tighten the lid.
4. Put a fourth Twinkie™ in another jar and cover it with water. Tighten the lid.
5. Line up your four experimental Twinkies™ .
6. Place them in locations around your home where they won't be disturbed, but also not forgotten. So, not on top of the fridge or in a closet.
7. Wait at least 30 days.

Step 5: Explore what happened

Look at the results. What do you notice?
Did the Twinkies™ rot?
Record your observations in a notebook.

Step 6: Share what happened

Share your results with others.

Chapter 6

Brain Dead

FEELING SLUGGISH?

Have you ever felt sluggish and dead tired like a zombie, wanting to sleep-in until noon? If so, maybe a sloth's life sounds appealing. Lazing around all day? Hanging out in trees and sleeping for hours on end? Sounds like a relaxing way of life! But before you pack your bags and head to the nearest rainforest, consider their reputation.

When French nature scientist Georges-Louis Leclerc first wrote about these unique mammals in 1749, he wasn't very kind. He said they were slow and probably dull-witted, too. And history has continued to misjudge these tree-loving dwellers, because of their sluggish ways, even today. An example is shown here in this joke.

What did the sloth chef use to cook her chilli in?

A slow cooker!

Zombie Bites

The Sleeping chironomid (informally known as a lake fly) knows a special hibernation-like trick called **cryptobiosis**–where it stays dormant, shutting down all signs of life. As a larva, this insect can stay in a sleep-like state for months. Like a zombie, it can survive in very harsh environments (e.g., insufferable cold or heat, extreme dryness, or lots of rain). As strange as it sounds, Scientists have discovered that the Sleeping chironomid can even live inside a vacuum cleaner!

Now before you poke fun at these slowpokes, you might want to consider why they move so slowly. Sloths do move at a sluggish rate. On an average day they travel only about 37 metres (41 yards—about the length of two bowling alley lanes if put together)! It all comes down to their diet. Sloths typically eat leaves, sometimes munching on the odd twig, but overall, they don't eat very much. Compared to other leaf-eating, tree dwellers like koalas, monkeys, and lemurs—sloths eat three times less! Having so little food contributes to a sluggish digestive system, which results in a very slow-moving sloth.

But don't let this laidback lifestyle fool you into feeling sorry for this idle creature. Scientists believe their slowness could be a survival skill. First, moving slowly requires less energy, meaning they don't need to spend as much time looking for food sources and they can survive on small amounts of leaves. Second, because sloths can't outrun predators, they rely on their camouflaged fur (caused by algae that grows on them) to help hide them. Moving very slowly allows sloths to go unnoticed as they travel from branch to branch, which works well because it is a good defence mechanism that keeps them safe.

These could be some of the reasons sloths have been around for 64 million years!

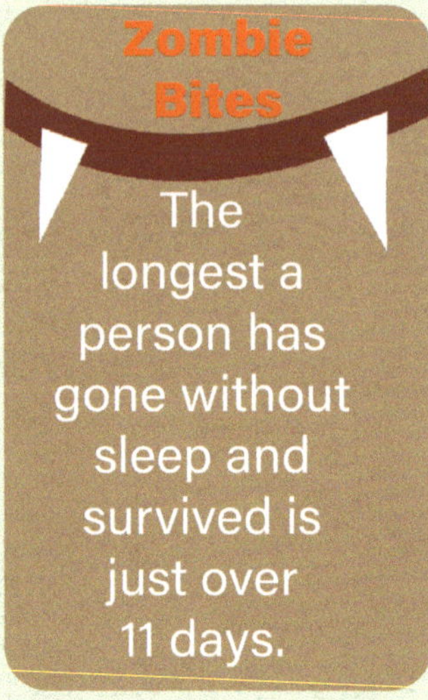

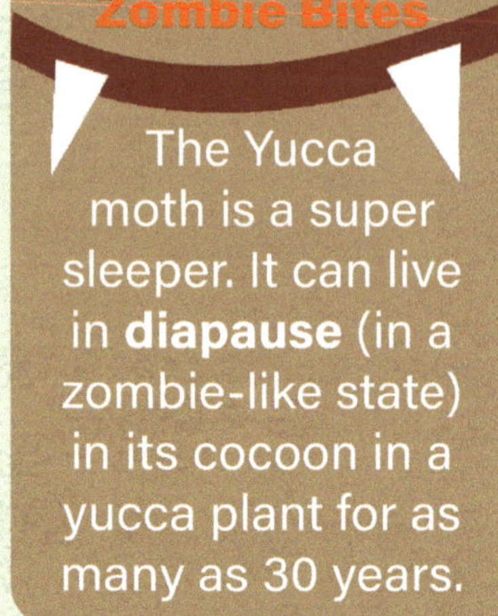

CATCHING ZZZ'S: ANIMAL ZZZ-OMBIES

Have you ever seen someone fall asleep, right in front of you? Maybe even as you're talking to them? Well, it's not that your conversations are boring; the person probably suffers from a sleep disorder called Narcolepsy. People with this disorder can unwillingly fall asleep doing routine activities, like eating, talking, or even while playing basketball! This condition affects brain signals that control our sleep-wake cycles, causing the brain to signal it's time to sleep at odd or random points during the day. The most common symptom is the uncontrollable need to sleep—instantly falling asleep anywhere, anytime. Researchers estimate approximately 5% of the population has this condition. It more often affects adult males.

Narcolepsy is rare in children, but our animal friends can suffer from this sleepy condition, too. Dogs, cats, mice and even horses have been known to have this disorder and many experience the same effects as humans. Imagine you're walking your dog and he unexpectedly takes a nap, right there on the sidewalk! These narcoleptic animals, big and small, might suddenly collapse and lose their ability to move. Just like humans, they can literally fall asleep, even while being physically active. Then suddenly they wake up and return to what they were doing, as if nothing ever happened. So, the next time you decide to go horse-back riding, hang on tight just in case your four-legged friend decides there's no more giddy-up to go!

Zombie Bites

Q fever is a bacterial illness that causes livestock (cattle, sheep, goats) to appear weak and tired. Once peed or pooped out of the animal, the bacteria can remain alive and contagious for several months or years.

DOG TIRED

Just when you thought it was safe to let your dog out into your backyard, you may want to stop and consider what might be growing there. That's right, Mother Nature has a few surprises up her sleeve—even for dogs! Every day, ordinary plants, flowers, and weeds can make your dog as dazed as a zombie! Read the passages below to help you investigate which plants will make your pup sluggish.

Can you spot the two safe, doggy sleep inducers?

Dandelions — Are related to sunflowers. Often referred to as a weed, these lawn invaders are very nutritious (even for dogs) and high in antioxidants. The leaves and stems may be used in a salad. When eaten, they can lower a human's blood pressure.

Pansies — Are known as a symbol of romantic affection. If you see them in cookies or on the top of a cake, don't worry because these flowers are edible for humans and dogs alike.

Chamomile — Can treat digestion problems, such as an upset stomach or diarrhea. It is one of the safest herbs you can offer your dog.

Mint — Both peppermint and spearmint have long been used to help relieve a human's upset stomach, as well as seasonal allergies. They are rich in nutrients and can help cover up bad breath—even stale doggy breath!

Roses — Are given as gifts to express feelings. They come in more than 2,500 colours, each with its own meaning. (i.e., yellow for friendship, red for love). The oil from the flower is used to make perfume, too. Roses are non-toxic for dogs, meaning that if your pup eats a small amount, it is unlikely to cause harm.

Passionflower — Has been used for centuries for its natural calming effects that can help with sleep. The white and purple climbing vine works to relieve stress, too! Passionflower is safe for dogs.

Echinacea — Is generally safe for dogs when used in moderation. For humans, Echinacea is an herb that is widely used to treat colds, flus, coughs, and sore throats. Herbalists believe the plant can boost our immune system, in other words, help fight off infections.

Answer Key:

1. Chamomile — Can be made into a tea. This plant contains Apigenin, a substance that can help people relax their muscles and get a good night's sleep.
2. Passionflower — As well as being a canine sleep inducer, it is often used for dogs who suffer from separation anxiety.

DEAD OR ASLEEP?

Do you have a green thumb (meaning you're an excellent gardener), or are you more of a plant killer? If greenery isn't your thing, then you may want to look into getting a Selaginella lepidophylla plant. It is also known as a Resurrection plant. Resurrection means bringing something back to life after it's dead—just like a zombie! This plant lives in the desert and as its nickname suggests, it dries up and by all appearances seems dead—like a dried out tumbleweed. Amazingly, all it takes is a little moisture to bring it back to life! Experts say a Resurrection plant can remain in a state of dormancy for long periods of time—several years without water! But as soon as water rehydrates the plant, it appears reborn. And when this happens, it returns to the land of the living.

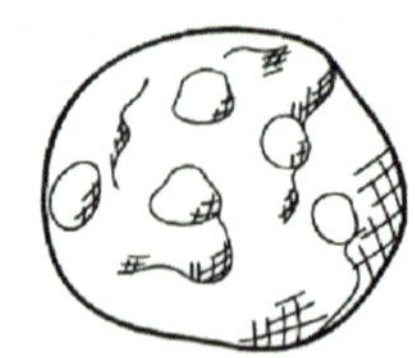

SLEEPY TREATS TO DIE FOR!

Chamomile Flower Shortbread Recipe
Follow these easy directions below.

Ingredients
50 grams (1.75 ounces) white sugar
100 grams (3.5 ounces) softened butter
150 grams (5 ounces) plain flour
1 egg
1.5 ml (1 tablespoon) milk
1.5 ml (1 tablespoon) fresh chamomile flowers

Instructions

1. Combine the sugar and butter in a food processor and mix.
2. Slowly add the flour until everything comes together in the form of a dough.
3. Place the dough on a clean work surface and roll it into a ball. Cover the ball in clear plastic wrap and chill in the refrigerator for 30 minutes.
4. Preheat the oven to 160 degrees Celsius (or 325 degrees Fahrenheit). Roll out the dough on a lightly floured surface and cut it into cookie shapes—like zombies!
5. In a separate bowl mix the egg and milk, creating an egg wash.
6. Brush the egg wash onto the cookies.
7. Place a chamomile flower on top of each cookie.
8. Sprinkle the cut-outs with sugar.
9. Ask a trusted adult to pop them into the oven for 10 to 12 minutes.
10. Share your sleep-easy treats with your gruesome gang of buddies.

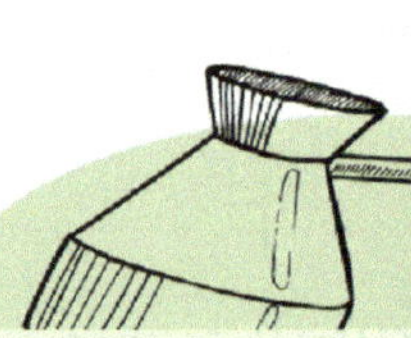

Chapter 7

Zombie Moves

WITHIN 'GAITED' COMMUNITIES

The word **gait** describes a living creature's manner of walking, including its posture, balance, coordination of muscles, and the length of its stride. Each person has a unique gait—distinct walking style. So do zombies! Most of them tend to lumber along clumsily on two legs, arms outstretched, reaching for their next victim. Some of them walk quickly, run, or even move awkwardly in quirky, jerky ways.

Humans and zombies use two legs to walk. We call that bipedal. Other creatures use four limbs to walk, such as cows, hippos, and giraffes. We call that quadrupedal. Some animals, like bears, gorillas, and even dogs (when they are performing tricks), who normally walk in quadrupedal ways, can also walk in bipedal ways.

For example, though bears usually walk on four legs, they also have the ability to walk only on their hind legs. Their bipedal way of walking looks like a flat-footed shuffle. They cannot walk on their back legs for long periods of time. Additionally, bears have been known to rise up on their hind legs to make themselves appear larger when they feel threatened.

Dogs do not naturally walk on two legs, because it is uncomfortable for them. However, some pet trainers do teach their dogs to stand tall or walk on their back legs.

There are other animals with interesting gaits. The crocodile shambles along with a wide stance on legs that are bent. Rabbits hop, using their powerful back legs to push them into the air. Cheetahs use slender limbs in coordination with their flexible spine to take long strides. Their galloping gait can help them reach speeds of up to 113 kilometres (70 miles) per hour. Given this rapid sprint, I'd take the lumbering human zombie!

TWITCHY MOVES

Have you ever felt your arm twitch? A small jerk in the muscle? In most cases, twitches are nothing out of the ordinary. They are caused by the involuntary tightening of muscles. You may have had a twitch in your eye, for example. These muscle spasms cannot be controlled—in other words, your body doesn't do them on purpose. They are caused by stress, eye strain, or lack of sleep. Or even something you drank, like caffeine—the chemical in coffee that can keep you awake. Usually eye twitches are not serious and they don't last very long.

Additionally, some people's muscles contract as they fall asleep. This is also common. Scientists call these twitches hypnic jerks. These involuntary body movements also happen in animals. Researchers believe that these sudden spasms occur when a body goes between alertness and sleep. It is possible that hypnic jerks are caused by the misfiring of nerves as sleep overtakes the body. Most people don't even remember these nighttime muscle contractions. Other people, however, might find the spasms annoying, especially if the twitches are strong enough to wake them.

Some types of twitches are more rare and can be more serious. For instance, people who have a condition called epilepsy may have seizures, which might require medical assistance or medication. These uncontrolled movements can occur in one area of the body (e.g., the legs, the arms, the face) or they can take over the entire body. A person having a seizure can be fully alert or can lose consciousness.

If you encounter someone having a seizure do not try to hold them still. Instead, clear away any nearby objects (like chairs or sharp items) so they do not bang or hurt themselves.

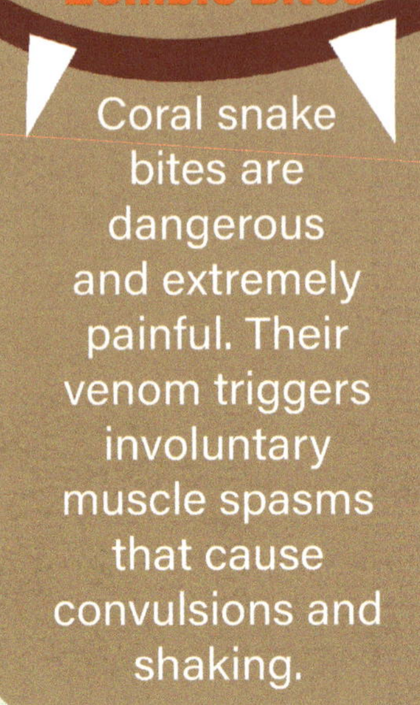

THE ZOMBIE SHUFFLE DANCE

Mix and match the different zombie-like movements to create your own dance.

Shrug shoulders

A shark does not have a tongue. Instead, it moves the muscles in its "**pectoral girdle**"—just like us shrugging our shoulders—to move food from its mouth to its stomach.

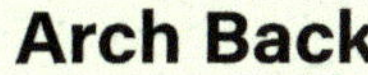

Arch Back

A gecko will arch its back when another gecko comes close in order to show dominance. This sign means, "BACK OFF!"

Hunch Back

A cat will curve its back when it stretches, but also when it is afraid.

Wave Legs and Arms Wildly

A male peacock spider will spread out its legs and wave them wildly to attract a mate and to avoid being eaten by the very female it is trying to impress.

Bob Head

A whooping crane does a mating ritual, in which it bobs and tosses its head to draw attention to itself.

Zombie Bites

Zombies in Chinese myths are called "Kuang Shi", meaning the hopping corpse.

STUMBLING AIMLESSLY

Zombies lumber, twitch, and slobber. This is because these fictional characters are said to have contracted an unnamed virus. But can a virus really influence an actual, living creature, making it sluggish, fidgety, and a drooling mess?

Yep. Viruses can make real-life creatures do strange things. Take **rabies**, for example. Rabies is an infectious disease that can affect all warm-blooded creatures, including animals and humans. The disease attacks the victim's brain and spinal cord. Read the encounter below to find out more.

It's a sunny afternoon and you and Rover are walking through the ravine, when all of a sudden you catch a foul whiff in the air. Pee-ew! What's that smell? Rover starts barking and tugging on his leash. Yikes, it's a skunk! But what's it doing out here in the daytime? You spot the cute little, black and white critter on the other side of the stream, but it's acting kind of weird. You watch as it paces back and forth, shaking and jittering. It seems nervous and confused, gnawing at the air, while aggressively making hissing sounds as it moves towards you and Rover. That's when you notice the drool dripping from its mouth. You realize it's time to skedaddle out of there, before you become its next victim!

This skunk has been infected with rabies, also known as the mad dog disease. It's a virus that slowly takes over a mammal's nervous system and causes its brain to swell. Any human or animal that gets bitten or scratched by this rabid skunk will begin to act like a zombie within days of being exposed to the virus. They may appear vacant-minded or could even become paralyzed. Or the opposite—they may become very aggressive, appearing to bite at imaginary things. They might have difficulty controlling their body movements. The telltale sign, though, is drool, dripping from the victim's mouth, perhaps making it look like the animal is foaming at the mouth. In North America, the most common victims of the rabies virus are skunks, raccoons, bats and foxes.

A MINDLESS WANDERER

It's a tale straight out of a horror novel. The story begins in Southeast Asia, with some hard-working carpenter ants. These busy insects spend most of each day building nests in the treetops, high among the branches.

On occasion an ant might venture down from the trees, to the ground, on the hunt for food. This is when the story takes a turn for the worse; one unsuspecting carpenter ant is about to become the host to a fungus called ophiocordyceps unilateralis, (commonly known as zombie-ant fungus). In order to reproduce, this fungus sends out spores that will eventually land on the insect and then soak into its body.

By the time the ant returns to its nest high up in the sunny treetops, the fungus is already invading its brain. The ant begins to shake and stumble about, losing control until it falls back down to the ground. Just what nature had planned. Now the ant appears to be wandering mindlessly, looking for its colony. Within the next few days, the zombie ant will be completely taken over as the fungus fills the brain and then grows right out of the ant's head.

TAKE ME TO YOUR LETTUCE?

Try this Brain Drain Science Experiment!
Can you change the direction of a colony of ants by encouraging them with food, making them veer off their pathway?

Try this outdoor experiment below.

What you'll need

Sugar
Honey
Cooking oil (such as olive oil or vegetable oil)
Food crumbs
Dead, decaying wood chips
Lettuce leaves—(to use as plates for the above ingredients)
You will also need a notebook in order to record your observations.

Step #1 Place equal amounts of the substances listed above on different lettuce leaves (a sugar leaf plate, a honey leaf plate, and so on).

Step # 2 Find an active anthill.

Step #3 Place your leaf plates around the anthill, putting them at an equal distance apart from one another.

Step #4 Sit back and watch. It won't take long before your dinner guests arrive!

Step #5 Which plate gets the most visitors? Are the ants taking some items away with them? What are they leaving behind?

Step #6 Choose the least popular item from your group of six. Pour sugar or honey on top of it. Are the ants taking the bait now? If they are, the ants are now under your control!

MOVING IN HORDES AND PACKS

According to science fiction authors, zombies have exceptional hearing and a sense of smell. Apparently a zombie can hear even the softest rustling of a person in hiding or the scream of a distant victim and will mindlessly follow the sound. They often gather to form a small pack that moves together. When the individual zombies join the already groaning and moaning pack, the sounds get louder. Those heightened noises attract even more zombies. Eventually, that pack becomes a huge, noise-making horde.

In real life, hunting in packs has proven to be an effective approach for wolves. Like fictional zombies, wolves also have a good sense of hearing, especially for high-pitched sounds. Their triangular-shaped ears can rotate independently. This ability allows them not only to pick up the sounds of the bellows and snorts of a herd of caribou up to 16 kilometres (10 miles) away, but it also helps individual wolves hear their own pack, find each other, and hunt together.

The pack attack has now begun. Individual wolves will make sounds, indicating to its pack that it is time to chase or circle the herd. The wolves seek out the weakest or youngest animal to attack. Caribou often make the mistake of running from the wolves. This helps the wolves; it means that the weakest caribou is singled out because it can't run as fast as its herd.

Once separated from its group, the wolves work together to bring their prey to the ground. Different wolves will attack the caribou's nose or rump area repeatedly, until the animal loses its balance and crashes down. Next, an **alpha** (pack leader) wolf pair (a male and a female), will tear into the caribou's flesh, killing it. The caribou will most likely die of shock or blood loss. Now, the alpha wolves get the privilege of feasting before the others. Only when the leaders are finished feeding on the prey, will the rest of the pack get to eat. For wolves, hunting in packs is a coordinated approach to meal-planning. It benefits the entire wolf pack, as each member gets food and protection.

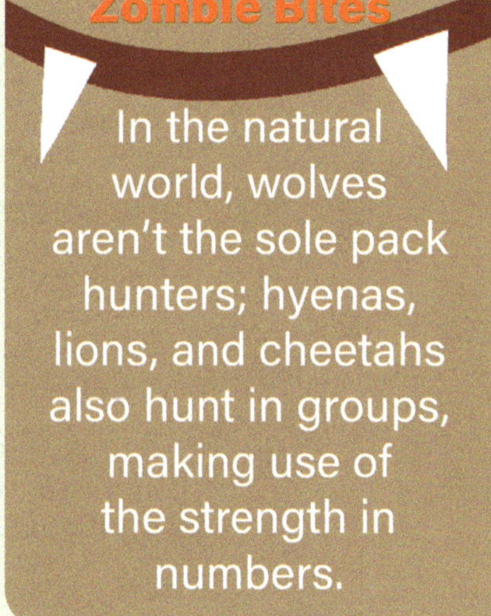

Chapter 8

Survival of the Fittest

THE LIVING DEAD

A scary fact about fictional zombies is that even after receiving a serious injury, these corpses live on. Maybe this is why zombies are called “the living dead”. According to the writers who make them up, zombies don’t die, unless they are fully decapitated.

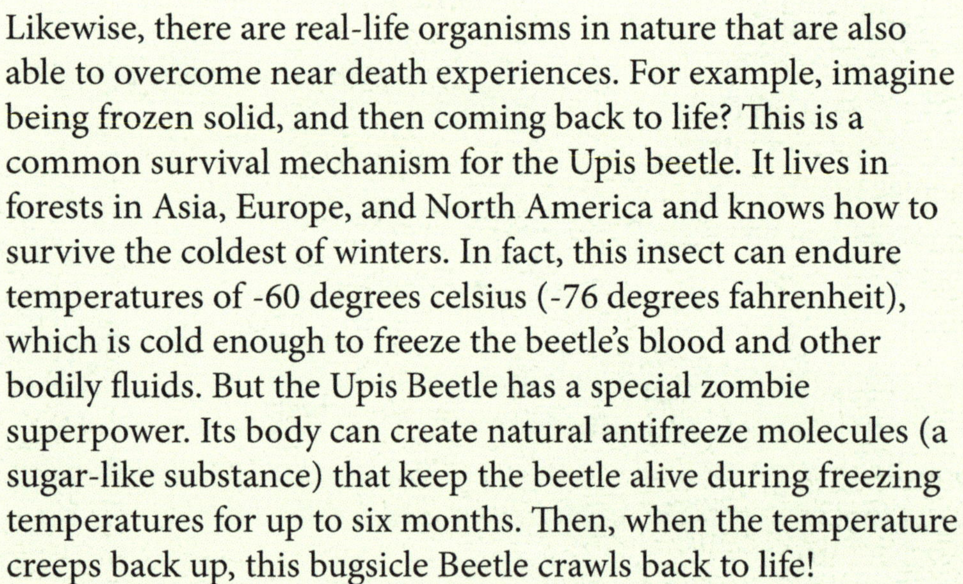

Likewise, there are real-life organisms in nature that are also able to overcome near death experiences. For example, imagine being frozen solid, and then coming back to life? This is a common survival mechanism for the Upis beetle. It lives in forests in Asia, Europe, and North America and knows how to survive the coldest of winters. In fact, this insect can endure temperatures of -60 degrees celsius (-76 degrees fahrenheit), which is cold enough to freeze the beetle’s blood and other bodily fluids. But the Upis Beetle has a special zombie superpower. Its body can create natural antifreeze molecules (a sugar-like substance) that keep the beetle alive during freezing temperatures for up to six months. Then, when the temperature creeps back up, this bugsicle Beetle crawls back to life!

The Wood frog is also able to survive the coldest Arctic temperatures. Its body produces a kind of preservative liquid sugar. This sugary substance floods into every cell within the frog’s body, attaching to water molecules so the frog doesn’t die, dry up, or freeze to death. Still living, the frog lies like a lifeless lump without any heartbeat, breathing, or muscle movement. But like a zombie, this frog regenerates itself! More specifically, the spring’s warmth thaws the frog. Once defrosted, the unharmed frog is ready to live and feast on insects once again.

It's hard to believe, but there are also real-life organisms too small to see with the human eye, that seemingly never die. They have existed for millions of years and can be found in oceans, forests, mines, mountains, and even glaciers all over the world. For instance, found in a mine in New Mexico, scientists discovered tiny but sturdy strains of bacteria. These microscopic zombie-like creatures were found inside a dried up chunk of tree sap that was nearly 250 million years old. The researchers thought the bacteria were dead. However, through careful **culturing** (creating environments/conditions that help things grow), the scientists brought four strains of these bacteria back to life. These are real-life examples of zombies that just won't stay dead!

IT'S ALIVE!

In the 1950s, people tried to sell children a new and unusual pet that had the death-defying traits of a zombie. They were aquatic critters called Sea Monkeys™. But they weren't monkeys at all. And they didn't live in the sea.

They were sold in a package as a magical dust and were actually Brine shrimp eggs (also called cysts). They could live on toy store shelves for up to two years. They could also survive in the wild unhatched (with the right amount of darkness, salt water, and with cool temperatures) for thousands of years. Once hatched, however, Brine shrimp only live for a year or two—and after they die, they do not come back to life.

WHO WILL SURVIVE?

In real-life and in fictional zombie stories, survival is often a struggle. Creatures regularly face-off to decide who rules in their world. While factors such as shape, size, fitness, and toughness can play key roles, it can be hard to predict who the winner will be.

From the list of opponents below, decide who is the fiercest competitor in a supreme showdown! There is an actual answer, according to scientists. But guess first and then look to see if you got the right answer.

1. Inland Taipan snake vs. Black mamba—one is the most venomous, the other is the most dangerous. The winner must strike first.

2. Praying mantis vs. Hummingbird—which wins in the end—speed or fighting skills?

3. Skunk vs. Racoon—the battle between these two late night scavengers is all teeth and claws!

4. Rat vs. Mouse—strength or speed? Which quality is the key to winning this battle?

5. Wolf vs. Moose—for these forest dwelling mammals, the victory goes to the one left standing. But between fierceness and strength, which will be the victor?

6. Great White Shark vs. Orca Whale—in the fight for ocean dominance, these massive animals are both fearsome predators.

7. Rhinoceros vs. Hippopotamus—the clash between these equally intimidating African beasts could be decided by the size and force of their bite.

1. Black Mamba 2. Praying Mantis 3. Raccoon 4. Rat
5. Moose 6. Orca Whale 7. Hippopotamus

MIKE, THE ZOMBIE-ROOSTER, LIVES ON!

On September 10, 1945, in the small farming community of Fruita, Colorado in the United States, a farmer named Lloyd Olsen set about the task of preparing the family dinner. Olsen went out to his barn, with his axe in hand, to select that night's meal. The farmer positioned a rooster and with a swift wack to its neck, the fatal blow was delivered. Or was it?

It turns out that Olsen's aim was a little off and the chop hit the bird higher up on its neck, leaving much of its brain stem still attached. It seemed that Mike, the bird, had other dinner plans (yes, that was the rooster's name). The rooster returned to hanging out with his feathered friends in the barnyard.

Olsen felt sorry for the bird. He placed Mike in a box and left him overnight on his porch. He was delighted the next morning to find Mike was still alive and Olsen realised this was a very special rooster! He and his wife began feeding Mike water and liquified food directly into his esophagus using an eyedropper, and then removing the mucus from his throat with a syringe. Before long, Headless Mike became famous! The Olsens took their death-defying rooster on tour—travelling across the United States, to country fairs and exhibitions, where Mike was a crowd favourite! Thousands of people came to see the zombie bird.

Mike lived for over a year before the most famous headless rooster took his last bow. Amazingly, in 2002, Mike's story made it into the Guinness Book of World Records!

Mike, the zombie, still survives today, in spirit anyway. Every May, in his hometown of Fruita, Colorado, an event is held, celebrating the local celebrity. I guess you could say, Mike still lives on!

Zombie Bites

The Tardigrade, or Water Bear, is a microscopic animal, so small you can't see it without a microscope. This tiny being is virtually indestructible. It can survive extreme dehydration and lose up to 97% of its body moisture and still survive.

10 "NEVER SAY DIE" FACTS ABOUT COCKROACHES

Cockroach! It's one of those words that gives you a creepy feeling when you hear it. Your imagination goes on high alert and you check the floor around you for this fast moving insect that seems almost impossible to kill. We've all heard the stories of these seemingly indestructible pests that carry disease, and some say, could even survive a nuclear blast. Well, with over 4,600 known species worldwide and a history that dates back over 300 million years on Earth, it's no wonder these speed demons are considered the true survivors.

Check out the zombie-like behaviours of these insect survivors.

Fact #1—Known to chomp off heads and limbs, fictional zombies could be considered cannibals. Likewise, cockroaches are real-life cannibalistic bugs! Yup, they will eat pretty much anything. They chow down on everything from fruit to hair, decaying meats to sweets, and even poop. Beware fellow roaches; they'll even eat you if their tummies are feeling empty!

Fact #2—Whereas a fictional zombie will die when decapitated, a cockroach can live without its head for a week or longer! These insects don't bleed and they breathe through their sides. So who needs a head? Without water, they too, will eventually die from dehydration or starve to death.

Fact #3—Depending on the imagination of writers who portray them, zombies have been known to swim and live underwater as they do not need oxygen to survive. Cockroaches, on the other hand, do need air to live but can hold their breath for a really long time—up to 40 minutes on land or 30 minutes underwater. That's a lot as the average human can only hold their breath for up to 90 seconds. Scientists believe they can do all this because they don't use their mouths to breathe. Instead they have small tubes called spiracles that are used to take water out of their bodies. Just like a faucet, they can turn it off when they are in drier environments.

Fact #4—Some writers portray zombies as speedy. In reality, cockroaches can run up to 5.5 kilometres (3.4 miles) per hour. For their size, that's fast. If they were the size of an average adult human, they'd be running about 354 kilometres (220 miles) per hour. That's nearly as fast as an F1 race car!

Fact #5—Baby cockroaches can run from the moment they are born. Talk about getting off to a fast start! Not only are they almost as fast as their parents, they are naturally just as clever at escaping or hiding.

Fact #6—Zombies are depicted as being able to live without food as they are not affected by starvation or dehydration. Cockroaches, however, need food, but can survive without it for a month. The main reason these real-life zombies can live without food for so long is that they are cold-blooded insects. Like all cold-blooded species they can control their body temperature. By lowering their body temperature, they conserve energy. This allows them to go for long periods of time without needing to feed.

Fact #7—Talk about a tight fit–cockroaches can squeeze through the tiniest cracks. They flatten their exoskeleton to ¼ of their body height and then spread their legs to the side, allowing them to slide in anywhere!

Fact #8—Cockroaches like to party!
Like fictional zombies that travel in hordes, cockroaches are social insects. They like to hang out in groups—called intrusions—and they certainly do intrude. Seems the more the merrier at their gatherings around your bathtub or kitchen sink. These crawling insects are nocturnal, so the party begins when the lights go out!

Fact #9—Cockroaches drink beer!
Studies show that cockroaches are beer lovers. Actually, it's not the alcohol that attracts them. Rather they are drawn to the sugars and **hops** (the flowers from a plant called Humulus lupulus) used in making the beer.

Fact #10—Cockroaches cannot survive a nuclear blast! It doesn't look good for fictional zombies either—however, enough hasn't been written by authors to say for sure. Regarding cockroaches, a myth began after the Second World War that these hardy insects could survive deadly nuclear blasts. In many studies since, experts have debunked this myth. Though they can stand higher levels of radiation than humans, they will die from the exposure to a blast.

HOW TO SURVIVE NATURAL DISASTERS (OR A ZOMBIE APOCALYPSE)

You've got four minutes to pack up and go! Although zombie apocalypses are fictional, the same basic survival methods can help you and your loved ones survive tornados, earthquakes, wildfires, snow storms, or floods.

Here's what you need to do before the trouble begins.

Tip#1 The best plan is to have a plan! Being prepared could be the key to staying alive.

Tip#2 Always have essentials on hand. Keep a supply of canned and dried foods, bottled water, and medical necessities.

Tip#3 Take shelter. Find a safe place to hide, preferably close to a fresh-water source.

Tip#4 Hold onto your cell phone. It's true! You may not be able to talk or text anyone, but you'll have GPS and a built-in flashlight.

Tip#5 A note to the wise. It's smart to have a disaster kit (e.g., candles, tools, can opener, blankets) ready for whatever nature may unleash!

Chapter 9

Zombie Allies

MAYBE, ZOMBIES AREN'T SO BAD?

They zombify humans, shuffle around, have insatiable appetites, and survive even the most dangerous situations. But what is their purpose?

By now you are probably thinking that a zombie's characteristics (e.g., flesh-eating, rotting, stumbling) are simply gross or dangerous. It's easy to see how, after reading this book, you might come to that conclusion. However, zombies aren't all bad. In fact, some of the things they do are celebrated in medicine, crime solving, health and beauty, and environmental fields. Believe it or not, zombie qualities can be helpful to humans. Read on to find out how humans interact with zombie-like creatures and make use of their peculiar behaviours to positively affect the world around them.

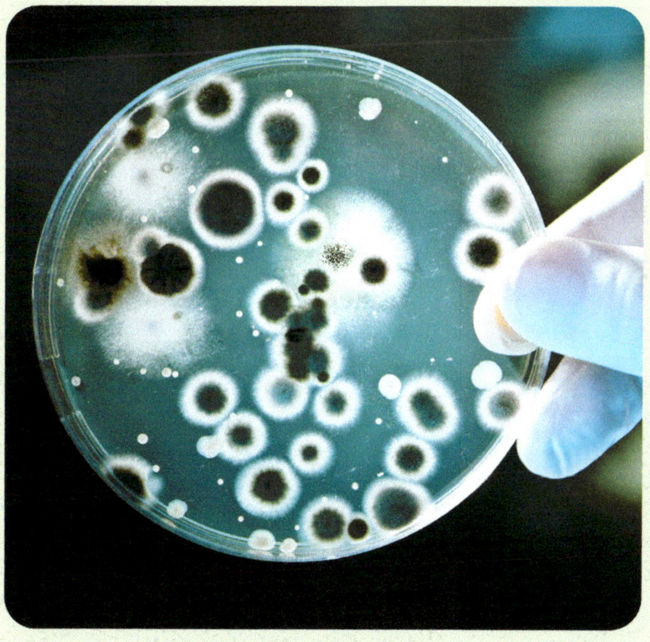

MUNCHING MAGGOTS

Maggots–the wormlike squigglers that grow to become flies—love to eat rotten things, including the flesh of dead animals, garbage, and poop. You might be thinking, "Ew!" However, as gross as this seems, these flesh-eating creepy crawlers aren't all bad. In fact, maggots play an important role in helping our planet. They are decomposers, meaning they break down tissues and put *nutrients* back into the soil. Additionally, they can be a food source for birds and rodents.

Maggots help humans in another way, too. For hundreds of years, some Indigenous peoples in North America and Australia have used maggots as a type of wound treatment.

You may be asking, "What do grub-like creatures have to do with repairing wounded tissues?" Imagine you have an infected cut that will not heal and is filled with pus. What could you do today to treat this wound?

One option is to visit a medical facility that offers **maggot** therapy. The medical staff will place the maggots on your wound. Soon these worm-like zombie-type creatures will burrow into and gnaw on the dying tissues. Their feasting will clean the cut in the process as their spit has antibacterial properties! Maggots to the rescue! Luckily, maggots only eat the rotting or infected flesh and leave healthy tissues alone. In this way, the maggots not only stop the spread of an infection, but they also clean up the injured area. Fortunately, patients cannot feel the wriggly *larvae*.

Once the wound has been cleaned by the **maggots**, some patients (including those with the disease called diabetes) are now ready to receive medical care such as *skin grafts* or other operations. Maggot therapy is becoming an increasingly popular healing procedure in modern medicine for soft tissue wounds as it saves infected limbs from amputation, and more importantly, it stops decay from spreading. And in this way, maggots save lives!

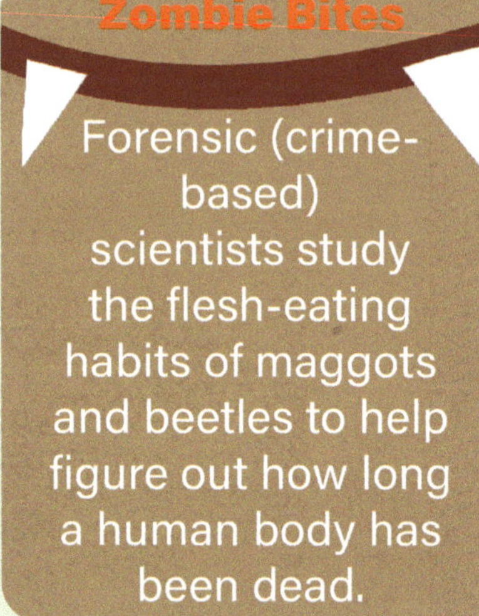

EYE SPY A ZOMBIE PLANT

Deadly Nightshade is an unwanted plant in most people's gardens. That is because it is poisonous to people and pets. Originally found in Europe and Asia, it has spread across the globe. This zombie plant invader takes its name very seriously–it's a killer! Everything about deadly nightshade is poisonous: from its dark berries to its purplish flowers. Eating one of its leaves can put victims into a *zombified* state, make them hallucinate, and twitch–or worse, it might kill them!

It sounds like a very strange thing to do. But, believe it or not, within the medical field, deadly nightshade is still used today! Some eye doctors use small quantities of deadly nightshade (which contains a chemical called atropine) to dilate pupils for eye examinations. The chemical also reduces swelling around the eyes, and can treat eye conditions such as "lazy eyes" (known as amblyopia). Perhaps when you look at this unwanted zombie-like invader in this way (with fresh eyes), this plant is wanted after all.

Given the dangers of Deadly Nightshade, it is hard to believe that women in the 1700s dropped the juice of its poisonous berries into their eyes. That's right! Some women believed that the eye drops made their faces more beautiful. In reality, the plant's **toxins** made their pupils appear bigger.

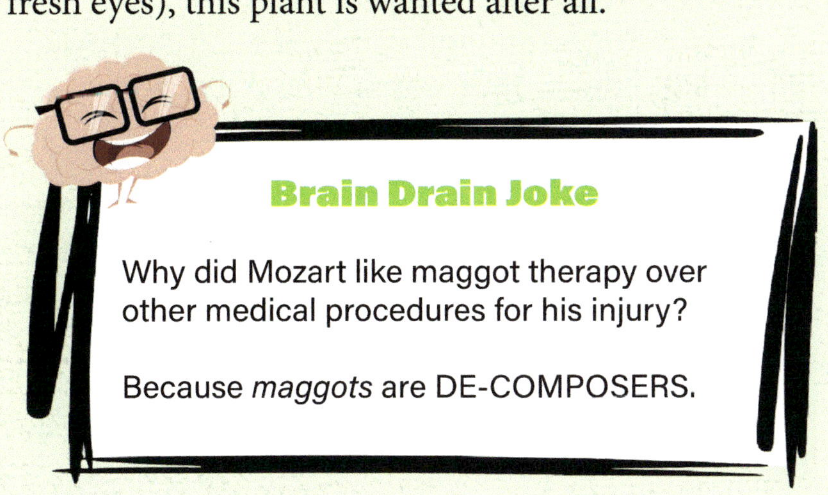

AGHHHHHH. I'M HUNGRY!

Like the zombies in movies, perhaps you never feel full. One cause of food cravings is *bacteria*. When gut bacteria are unbalanced, a person may find themselves wanting to eat a whole pizza or an entire cake! Too many gut microbes (especially "bad bacteria") can also make you crave sweets and junk food. In this way, these microscopic "zombies" might be messing with your mind.

Though more research is needed on how these small organisms can influence a person's eating behaviours, scientists do know that more than a hundred trillion microbes share your meals with you. Microbes like **bacteria**, **fungi**, and viruses make up what scientists call "the human microbiome". Some of these microbes were passed on to you when you were born. Others developed as you grew older.

Luckily, many of these tiny organisms also help with digestion and the way your body absorbs *nutrients*. Others produce hormones that tell your brain when your stomach is full. So when that insatiable hunger takes hold and the zombie-eating habits take over, remember your gut may be the problem… and also the solution.

YOU'RE A ZOMBIE: YOU HAVEN'T AGED A BIT

Botulism is a rare but serious illness that people can get when they eat foods that have not been properly canned. This is because improperly preserved food causes bacterial growth. These *bacteria* (called clostridium botulinum) can produce dangerous substances called *toxins*. Once poisoned with the clostridium botulinum toxin, people can appear zombie-like, with droopy eyelids, facial weakness, abdominal cramps, and sluggish body movements.

So it may be hard to believe that people inject, using needles, tiny amounts of the clostridium botulinum toxin (shortened to Botox) into their faces in order to reduce the appearance of wrinkles. However, as unbelievable as it seems, it is true! In fact, a current plastic surgery statistics report said that this industry is growing and, in recent years, encountered a 4% increase from previous years!

SURVIVING DEATH?

In movies and books, zombies rarely die. They live on and on. What a sturdy lot! Imagine if humans could bottle up that longevity!

Though it is not possible for humans, at this point, to live past the age of 125, there are some medical procedures that can help to extend the lives of humans. Some blood transfusions, for example, can help people live longer. When people lose blood–for instance, when they've been in an accident–they can suffer from lower oxygen levels. It is estimated that more than 4.5 million people require blood transfusions every year in Canada and the United States. These transfused, healthy red blood cells can live in a person's circulatory system for 120 days and can offer immediate relief and a better quality of life.

Heart, liver, lung, and pancreas organ transplants are another way that doctors can save and extend their patients' lives. Transplants need to happen quickly because organs do not survive for long outside of a human body. However, once the transplant has occurred and when the person has ongoing medical care, the organs can potentially survive for decades, giving patients a second chance at life.

You're a Zombie Survivor!

This book's information on how nature's zombies fit into the natural world may have scared you, grossed you out, or given you food for thought. But you've made it–to the end of the book! Congratulations! You are a ZOMBIE SURVIVOR!

As you move beyond this book, returning to your daily life, remember what these unique zombie qualities bring to our natural world. Perhaps, with additional scientific research, curiosity, and critical thought, you might someday be the expert who stumbles into new fields, invades old ideas, devours new information, extends life spans for various species, and even teaches humans how to defy death!

Index

A

amber snail 13, 18

B

bacteria 13, 16, 19, 28, 35, 43, 55, 62, 64, 68
barnacle 12, 68
botflies 29

C

catalyst 37, 68
crickets 29
cockroaches 30, 58-59
cysts 30, 55, 68

D

deadly nightshade 13, 63,

E

E coli 13, 16, 68
ecosystem 16, 68
enzymes 37, 38, 68
eyestalks 18, 68

F

flukes 12, 13, 29, 68
food web 17, 19, 68

G

gait 47, 68
guinea worms 12, 13, 29

H

hairworms 12
host 12, 13, 26, 27, 29, 31, 51, 59

I

inland taipan snake 13, 56

J

jewel wasp 13, 30

K

komodo dragons 12, 13, 14, 17, 35

L

larvae 18, 25, 26, 27, 29, 30, 41, 62, 69

M

moths 13, 42

N

nutrients 16, 44, 62, 64, 69

O

oxidize 37, 69

P

pathogens 28, 31, 69
parasites 12, 13, 16, 18, 25, 26, 28, 30, 31, 69, 70, 71
pica 20, 69

Q

Q fever 13, 43

R

rabies 13, 14, 50, 69
rot 7, 11, 12, 13, 14, 15, 23, 33, 35, 36, 37, 39-40, 61, 62, 69

S

seizure 48
sloths 13, 41-42,

T

ticks 12, 21, 34
toxins 63, 64, 69

U

urine 30, 33

V

virus 7, 13, 16, 25, 28, 50, 64, 69

W

wolves 53, 56, 68

X

Y

yeast 13

Z

zombie deer disease 28
zombified 7, 9, 10, 13, 18 25, 27, 29, 30, 32, 63, 69

Alpha: the top dog in a wolf pack.

Apocalypse: a catastrophic event that is so terrible it could bring the world to an end.

Bacteria: not visible to the human eye, these single celled, living microscopic organisms, can be found in all natural environments.

Barnacle: a small shelled creature, found in the water that attaches itself to surfaces like rocks, boats, and whales.

Catalyst: a substance that can increase the rate of a chemical reaction without being consumed or changed by the reaction.

Cryptobiosis: a sleeplike state similar to hibernation.

Culturing: to grow tissues or microorganisms in a controlled environment.

Cysts: is a sac of air, liquid or pus, found in different parts of a body.

Diapause: a pause in an animal's growth.

Diurnal: animals that are active during the day and like to sleep at night.

E coli: this bacteria normally breaks down food in the intestine, but also can live in contaminated food or water and spread disease.

Ecosystem: a network of organisms interacting within a physical environment. (e.g.,marine, desert, rainforest, freshwater)

Enzymes: are proteins that help speed up the chemical reactions in the body.

Eyestalks: an antenna-like structure found on a snail that has a compound eye on its tip.

Fluke: a parasitic flatworm, often found in water.

Food web: interconnected food chains that are part of an ecosystem.

Fungus/Fungi: is a simple organism that is living, but is neither a plant nor an animal.

Gait: the ways an animal or person runs or walks.

Hops: the dried flowers of the twining plant, used in making beer.

Host: a plant or animal which provides a food source and/or habitat for a parasite.

Larva: a young, wingless insect that hatches from an egg, before it turns into an adult.

Maggot: a soft-bodied, legless grub that is the larva of a fly (housefly).

Microorganisms: are living things that can only be viewed through a microscope.

Nutrient: a substance that supplies nourishment essential for growth and maintaining life.

Oxidizing: a chemical reaction that happens when a physical material/substance (e.g., metal) comes into contact with oxygen.

Parasites: living creatures that feed on other creatures (their host) in order to survive.

Pathogens: tiny organisms that cause infectious disease such as viruses or bacteria outbreaks.

Pectoral girdle: a ring of bones that support a shark's (arm-like) fins.

Pica: an eating disorder that causes people to eat things that are not normally considered food.

Preservatives: substances added to food to keep them from rotting.

Proteins: nutrients that build and support the tissues of our bodies, like muscles or bones.

Rabies: is a serious viral infection that attacks the nervous system. It is usually transmitted through a bite from an infected animal.

Skin Graft: a surgical operation, where healthy skin is transplanted to a new place on the body.

Stupefaction: to be in a state of uncontrollable numbness—unable to think.

Toxin: a poisonous substance that can be produced by living things.

Zombified: to transform a living, functioning being into a zombie.

References

YOUTUBE VIDEOS

Cordyceps: attack of the killer fungi - Planet Earth Attenborough BBC wildlife

Rats attacking cats - World's Weirdest Events: Episode 7 Preview - BBC One

'Zombie' Parasite Takes Over Insects Through Mind Control | National Geographic
https://www.enkivillage.org/how-long-does-it-take-for-a-body-to-decompose.html

https://www.youtube.com/watch?v=pM15UYEoOlE&ab_channel=AbraarBawazeerHindi

BOOKS AND MAGAZINES

Davies, N., & Layton, N.(2007). *What's eating you?* Cambridge, MA: Candlewick Press.

Drisdelle, R. (2010). *Parasites: Tales of humanity's unwelcome guests.* Berkeley, CA: University of California Press.

Gussoni, C., & McDonnell, L. (2008). *The awesome book of bugs.* Philadelphia. PA: Running Press Kids.

Hirschmann, C. (2013). *Real life zombies.* Scholastic Inc.

Johnson, R. J. (2013). *Zombie makers: True stories of nature's undead.* Minneapolis, MN: Millbrook Press.

Masoff, J. & Sirrell, T. (2006). *Oh yikes! History's grossest, wackiest moments.* New York, NY: Workman Publishing.

McAuliffe, K. (2017). *This is your brain on Parasites.* Boston, MA: HMH Books.

National Geographic (2014). *Real Zombies.*

Stiefel, C. (2018). *Animal zombies!* Washington, D.C.: National Geographic Kids.

Szpirglas, J., & Cho, M. (2004). *Gross universe.* Toronto, ON: Maple Tree Press.

Woodword, J. (2002). *Pesky parasites.* Chicago, IL: Heinemann Library.

Author Bios

Dr. Kari-Lynn Winters is a full professor, award-winning Canadian children's author, performer, and playwright. Her children's writing has been nominated for many prestigious awards. She currently teaches drama-in-education, dance-in-education, and language arts to teacher candidates at Brock University in the Faculty of Education. Holding degrees from UBC, OISE/UT, Brock University, and the National Theatre School in literacy education, teacher education, and the arts, her research interests include STEAM, refugee education, mental health, social equity, body image, embodied pedagogies, children's literature, drama, and multimodal literacies.

Catherine Rondina is a published author, educator and library assistant,whose writing career spans more than 30 years in the industry. Her non-fiction books have won the Silver Birch Award (2012 and 2019), the Hackmatack Award (2012), and the Teacher's Choice Award in the United States (2008). She has also been nominated for the Rocky Mountain Book Award (2020). In addition to being an educator with George Brown College in Toronto (2007-2018), Catherine has published educational anthologies from grades 4-12, for publishers like, Nelson Education, Prentice Hall Ginn, Pearson Education, and Gage.

Catherine takes great pride in her more than 37 years with the Toronto Public Library. Her career, as a Library Assistant, has allowed her to work in programming and literacy for both young adults and children.